Margaret Atwood is the author of more than forty works, including fiction, poetry and critical essays, and her books have been published in over thirty-five countries. Of her novels, *The Blind Assassin* won the 2000 Booker Prize and *Alias Grace* won the Giller Prize in Canada and the Premio Mondello in Italy. Margaret Atwood's most recent novel is *MaddAddam* (2013). In 2005 she was the recipient of the Edinburgh Book Festival Enlightenment Award, for a distinguished contribution to world literature and thought. In 2008, Margaret Atwood was awarded the Prince of Asturias Prize for Literature in Spain. She lives in Toronto.

For more information, visit www.margaretatwood.ca

ALSO BY MARGARET ATWOOD

MARGARET ATWOOD

GOOD BONES

virago

VIRAGO

Published by Virago Press in 1993
First published in Great Britain by Bloomsbury Publishing Ltd in 1992
This edition published by Virago Press in 2010
Reprinted 2013, 2014 (twice)

A CIP catalogue record for this book
is available from the British Library.

ISBN 978-1-84408-692-4

Typeset in Bembo by M Rules
Printed and bound in Great Britain by
Clays Ltd, St Ives plc

Papers used by Virago are from well-managed forests
and other responsible sources.

MIX
Paper from
responsible sources
FSC
www.fsc.org   FSC® C104740

Virago Press
An imprint of
Little, Brown Book Group
100 Victoria Embankment
London EC4Y 0DY

An Hachette UK Company
www.hachette.co.uk

www.virago.co.uk

CONTENTS

For G., as always, and for the two Angelas

GOOD BONES

GOOD BONES

Bad News

The red geraniums fluorescing on the terrace, the wind swaying the daisies, the baby's milk-fed eyes focusing for the first time on a double row of beloved teeth – what is there to report? Bloodlessness puts her to sleep. She perches on a rooftop, her brass wings folded, her head with its coiffure of literate serpents tucked beneath the left one, snoozing like a noon pigeon. There's nothing to do but her toenails. The sun oozes across the sky, the breezes undulate over her skin like warm silk stockings, her heart beats with the systole and diastole of waves on the breakwater, boredom creeps over her like vines.

She knows what she wants: an event, by which she means a slip of the knife, a dropped wineglass or bomb, something broken. A little acid, a little gossip, a little hi-tech megadeath: a sharp thing that will wake her up. Run a tank over the geraniums, turn the wind up to hurricane so the daisies' heads tear off and hurtle through the air like bullets, drop the baby from the balcony and watch the mother swan-dive after him, with her snarled Ophelia hair and addled screams.

The melon-burst, the tomato-coloured splatter – now that's a story! She's awake now, she sniffs the air, her wings are spread for flight. She's hungry, she's on the track, she's howling like a siren and she's got your full attention.

No news is good news, everyone knows that. You know it, too, and you like it that way. When you're feeling bad she scratches at your window, and you let her in. *Better them than you*, she whispers in your ear. You settle back in your chair, folding the rustling paper.

The Little Red Hen Tells All

Everyone wants in on it. Everyone! Not just the cat, the pig and the dog. The horse too, the cow, the rhinoceros, the orang-outang, the horn-toad, the wombat, the duckbilled platypus, you name it. There's no peace any more and all because of that goddamn loaf of bread.

It's not easy, being a hen.

You know my story. Probably you had it told to you as a shining example of how you yourself ought to behave. Sobriety and elbow-grease. Do it yourself Then invest your capital. Then collect. I'm supposed to be an illustration of *that*? Don't make me laugh.

5

I found the grain of wheat, true. So what? There are lots of grains of wheat lying around. Keep your eyes to the grindstone and you could find a grain of wheat, too. I saw one and picked it up. Nothing wrong with that. Finders keepers. A grain of wheat saved is a grain of wheat earned. Opportunity is bald behind.

Who will help me plant this grain of wheat? I said. *Who? Who?* I felt like a goddamn owl.

Not me, not me, they replied. *Then I'll do it myself,* I said, as the nun quipped to the vibrator. Nobody was listening, of course. They'd all gone to the beach.

Don't think it didn't hurt, all that rejection. Brooding in my nest of straw, I cried little red hen tears. Tears of chicken blood. You know what that looks like, you've eaten enough of it. Makes good gravy.

So, what were my options? I could have eaten that grain of wheat right away. Done myself a nutritional favour. But instead I planted it. Watered it. Stood guard over it night and day with my little feathered body.

So it grew. Why not? So it made more grains of wheat. So I planted those. So I watered those. So I ground them into flour. So I finally got enough for a loaf of bread. So I baked it. You've seen the pictures, me in my little red hen apron, holding the loaf with its plume of aroma in between the tips of my wings, smiling away. I smile in all the pictures, as much as you can smile, with a beak. Whenever they said *Not me*, I smiled. I never lost my temper.

Who will help me eat this loaf of bread? I said. *I will*, said the cat, the dog and the pig. *I will*, said the antelope. *I will*, said the yak. *I will*, said the five-lined skink. *I will*, said the pubic louse. They meant it, too. They held out their paws, hooves, tongues, claws, mandibles, prehensile tails. They drooled at me with their eyes. They whined. They shoved petitions through my mail slot. They became depressed. They accused me of selfishness. They developed symptoms. They threatened suicide. They said it was my fault, for having a loaf of bread when they had none. Every single one of them, it seemed, needed that goddamn loaf of bread more than I did.

You can bake more, they said.

———

So then what? I know what the story says, what I'm supposed to have said: *I'll eat it myself, so kiss off.* Don't believe a word of it. As I've pointed out, I'm a hen, not a rooster.

Here, I said. *I apologize for having the idea in the first place. I apologize for luck. I apologize for self-denial. I apologize for being a good cook. I apologize for that crack about nuns. I apologize for that crack about roosters. I apologize for smiling, in my smug hen apron, with my smug hen beak. I apologize for being a hen.*

Have some more.

Have mine.

Gertrude Talks Back

I always thought it was a mistake, calling you Hamlet. I mean, what kind of a name is that for a young boy? It was your father's idea. Nothing would do but that you had to be called after him. Selfish. The other kids at school used to tease the life out of you. The nicknames! And those terrible jokes about pork.

I wanted to call you George.

I am *not* wringing my hands. I'm drying my nails.

Darling, please stop fidgeting with my mirror. That'll be the third one you've broken.

Yes, I've seen those pictures, thank you very much. I *know* your father was handsomer than Claudius. High brow, aquiline nose and so on, looked great in uniform. But handsome isn't everything, especially in a man, and far be it from me to speak ill of the dead, but I think it's about time I pointed out to you that your Dad just wasn't a whole lot of fun. Noble, sure, I grant you. But Claudius, well, he likes a drink now and then. He appreciates a decent meal. He enjoys a laugh, know what I mean? You don't always have to be tiptoeing around because of some holier-than-thou principle or something.

By the way, darling, I wish you wouldn't call your step-dad *the bloat king*. He does have a slight weight problem, and it hurts his feelings.

The rank sweat of a *what*? My bed is certainly not *enseamed*, whatever that might be! A nasty sty, indeed! Not that it's any of your business, but I change those sheets twice a week, which is more than you do, judging from that student slum pigpen in Wittenberg. I'll certainly never visit you *there* again without prior warning! I see that laundry of yours when you bring it home, and not often enough either, by a long shot!

Only when you run out of black socks.

And let me tell you, everyone sweats at a time like that, as you'd find out very soon if you ever gave it a try. A real girlfriend would do you a heap of good. Not like that pasty-faced what's-her-name, all trussed up like a prize turkey in those touch-me-not corsets of hers. If you ask me, there's something off about that girl. Borderline. Any little shock could push her right over the edge.

Go get yourself someone more down-to-earth. Have a nice roll in the hay. Then you can talk to me about nasty sties.

No, darling, I am not *mad* at you. But I must say you're an awful prig sometimes. Just like your Dad. *The Flesh*, he'd say. You'd think it was dog dirt. You can excuse that in a young person, they are always so intolerant, but in someone his age it was getting, well, very hard to live with, and that's the understatement of the year.

Some days I think it would have been better for both of us if you hadn't been an only child. But you realize who

11

you have to thank for *that*. You have no idea what I used to put up with. And every time I felt like a little, you know, just to warm up my ageing bones, it was like I'd suggested murder.

Oh! You think *what*? You think Claudius murdered your Dad? Well, no wonder you've been so rude to him at the dinner table!

If I'd known *that*, I could have put you straight in no time flat.

It wasn't Claudius, darling.

It was me.

There Was Once

— There was once a poor girl, as beautiful as she was good, who lived with her wicked stepmother in a house in the forest.

— Forest? *Forest* is passé, I mean, I've had it with all this wilderness stuff. It's not a right image of our society, today. Let's have some *urban* for a change.

— There was once a poor girl, as beautiful as she was good, who lived with her wicked stepmother in a house in the suburbs.

— That's better. But I have to seriously query this word *poor*.

— But she *was* poor!

— Poor is relative. She lived in a house, didn't she?

— Yes.

— Then socio-economically speaking, she was not poor.

— But none of the money was *hers*! The whole point of the story is that the wicked stepmother makes her wear old clothes and sleep in the fireplace—

— Aha! They had a *fireplace*! With *poor*, let me tell you, there's no fireplace. Come down to the park, come to the subway stations after dark, come down to where they sleep in cardboard boxes, and I'll show you *poor*!

— There was once a middle-class girl, as beautiful as she was good—

— Stop right there. I think we can cut the *beautiful*, don't you? Women these days have to deal with too many intimidating physical role models as it is, what

14

with those bimbos in the ads. Can't you make her, well, more average?

— There was once a girl who was a little overweight and whose front teeth stuck out, who—

— I don't think it's nice to make fun of people's appearances. Plus, you're encouraging anorexia.

— I wasn't making fun! I was just describing—

— Skip the description. Description oppresses. But you can say what colour she was.

— What colour?

— You know. Black, white, red, brown, yellow. Those are the choices. And I'm telling you right now, I've had enough of white. Dominant culture this, dominant culture that—

— I don't know what colour.

— Well, it would probably be *your* colour, wouldn't it?

— But this isn't *about* me! It's about this girl—

— Everything is about you.

— Sounds to me like you don't want to hear this story at all.

— Oh well, go on. You could make her ethnic. That might help.

— There was once a girl of indeterminate descent, as average-looking as she was good, who lived with her wicked—

— Another thing. *Good* and *wicked*. Don't you think you should transcend those puritanical judgemental moralistic epithets? I mean, so much of that is conditioning, isn't it?

— There was once a girl, as average-looking as she was well-adjusted, who lived with her stepmother, who was not a very open and loving person because she herself had been abused in childhood.

— Better. But I am so *tired* of negative female images! And stepmothers – they always get it in the neck! Change it to step*father*, why don't you? That would make more sense anyway, considering the bad behaviour you're about to describe. And throw in some whips and chains. We all know what those twisted, repressed, middle-aged men are like—

— *Hey, just a minute!* I'm *a middle-aged*—

— Stuff it, Mister Nosy Parker. Nobody asked you to stick in your oar, or whatever you want to call that thing. This is between the two of us. Go on.

— There was once a girl—

— How old was she?

— I don't know. She was young.

— This ends with a marriage, right?

— Well, not to blow the plot, but – yes.

— Then you can scratch the condescending paternalistic terminology. It's *woman*, pal. *Woman*.

— There was once—

— What's this *was*, *once*? Enough of the dead past. Tell me about *now*.

— There—

— So?

— So, what?

— So, why not *here*?

Unpopular Gals

Everyone gets a turn, and now it's mine. Or so they used to tell us in kindergarten. It's not really true. Some get more turns than others, and I've never had a turn, not one! I hardly know how to say *I*, or *mine*; I've been *she, her, that one*, for so long.

I haven't even been given a name; I was always just *the ugly sister*; put the stress on *ugly*. The one the other mothers looked at, then looked away from and shook their heads gently. Their voices lowered or ceased alto-gether when I came into the room, in my pretty dresses, my face leaden and scowling. They tried to think of something to say that would redeem the situation –

19

Well, she's certainly strong — but they knew it was useless.
So did I.

You think I didn't hate their pity, their forced kindness?
And knowing that no matter what I did, how virtuous
I was, or hardworking, I would never be beautiful. Not
like her, the one who merely had to sit there to be
adored. You wonder why I stabbed the blue eyes of my
dolls with pins and pulled their hair out until they were
bald? Life isn't fair. Why should I be?

As for the prince, you think I didn't love him? I loved
him more than she did; I loved him more than anything.
Enough to cut off my foot. Enough to murder. Of
course I disguised myself in heavy veils, to take her place
at the altar. Of course I threw her out the window and
pulled the sheets up over my head and pretended to be
her. Who wouldn't, in my position?

But all my love ever came to was a bad end. Red-hot
shoes, barrels studded with nails. That's what it feels like,
unrequited love.

She had a baby, too. I was never allowed.

Everything you've ever wanted, I wanted also.

2

A libel action, that's what I'm thinking. Put an end to this nonsense. Just because I'm old and live alone and can't see very well, they accuse me of all sorts of things. Cooking and eating children, well, can you imagine? What a fantasy, and even if I did eat just a few, whose fault was it? Those children were left in the forest by their parents, who fully intended them to die. Waste not, want not, has always been my motto.

Anyway, the way I see it, they were an offering. I used to be given grown-ups, men and women both, stuffed full of seasonal goodies and handed over to me at seed-time and harvest. The symbolism was a little crude perhaps, and the events themselves were some might say – lacking in taste, but folks' hearts were in the right place. In return, I made things germinate and grow and swell and ripen.

Then I got hidden away, stuck into the attic, shrunken and parched and covered up in fusty draperies. Hell, I used to have breasts! Not just two of them. Lots. Ever wonder why a third tit was the crucial test, once, for women like me?

Or why I'm so often shown with a garden? A wonderful garden, in which mouth-watering things grow. Mulberries. Magic cabbages. Rapunzel, whatever that is. And all those pregnant women trying to clamber over the wall, by the light of the moon, to munch up my fecundity, without giving anything in return. Theft, you'd call it, if you were at all open-minded.

That was never the rule in the old days. Life was a gift then, not something to be stolen. It was my gift. By earth and sea I bestowed it, and the people gave me thanks.

3

It's true, there are never any evil stepfathers. Only a bunch of lily-livered widowers, who let me get away with murder vis-à-vis their daughters. Where are they when I'm making those girls drudge in the kitchen, or sending them out into the blizzard in their paper dresses? Working late at the office. Passing the buck. Men! But if you think they knew nothing about it, you're crazy.

The thing about those good daughters is, they're so *good*. Obedient and passive. Snivelling, I might add. No get-up-and-go. What would become of them if it weren't for me? Nothing, that's what. All they'd ever do is the housework, which seems to feature largely in these stories. They'd marry some peasant, have seventeen kids, and get 'A dutiful wife' engraved on their tombstones, if any. Big deal.

I stir things up, I get things moving. 'Go play in the traffic,' I say to them. 'Put on this paper dress and look for strawberries in the snow.' It's perverse, but it works. All they have to do is smile and say hello and do a little more housework, for some gnomes or nice ladies or whatever, and bingo, they get the king's son and the palace, and no more dishpan hands.

Whereas all I get is the blame.

God knows all about it. No Devil, no Fall, no Redemption. Grade Two arithmetic.

You can wipe your feet on me, twist my motives around all you like, you can dump millstones on my head and drown me in the river, but you can't get me out of the story. I'm the plot, babe, and don't ever forget it.

Let Us Now Praise Stupid Women

—the airheads, the bubblebrains, the ditzy blondes:
the headstrong teenagers too dumb to listen to
   their mothers:
all those with mattress stuffing between their ears,
all the lush hostesses who tell us to have a good day,
   and give us the wrong change, while checking
   their Big Hair in the mirror,
all those who dry their freshly-shampooed poodles
   in the microwave,
and those whose boyfriends tell them chlorophyll
   chewing gum is a contraceptive, and who believe
   it;
all those with nervously bitten fingernails because
   they don't know whether to pee or get off the
   pot,

25

all those who don't know how to spell the word
    pee,
all those who laugh good-naturedly at stupid jokes
    like this one, even though they don't get the
    point.

They don't live in the real world, we tell ourselves
    fondly: but what kind of criticism is that?
If they can manage not to live in it, good for
    them. We would rather not live in it either,
    ourselves.
And in fact they don't live in it, because such
    women are fictions: composed by others, but
    just as frequently by themselves,
though even stupid women are not so stupid as
    they pretend: they pretend for love.
Men love them because they make even stupid
    men feel smart: women for the same reason,
and because they are reminded of all the stupid
    things they have done themselves,
but mostly because without them there would be
    no stories.

No stories! No stories! Imagine a world without
    stories!

But that's exactly what you would have, if all the
    women were wise.

The Wise Virgins keep their lamps trimmed and
    filled with oil, and the bridegroom arrives, in
    the proper way, knocking at the front door, in
    time for his dinner;

no fuss, no muss, and also no story at all.

What can be told about the Wise Virgins, such
    bloodless paragons?

They bite their tongues, they watch their smart
    mouths, they sew their own clothing,

they achieve professional recognition, they do
    every right thing without effort.

Somehow they are insupportable: they have no
    narrative vices:

their wise smiles are too knowing, too knowing
    about us and our stupidities.

We suspect them of having mean hearts.

They are far too clever, not for their own good but
    for ours.

The Foolish Virgins, on the other hand, let their
    lamps go out:
and when the bridegroom turns up and rings the
    doorbell,
they are asleep in bed, and he has to climb in
    through the window:
and people scream and fall over things, and identi-
    ties get mistaken,
and there's a chase scene, and breakage, and much
    satisfactory uproar:
none of which would have happened if these
    girls hadn't been several bricks short of a
    load.

Ah the Eternal Stupid Woman! How we enjoy
    hearing about her:
as she listens to the con-artist yarns of the plausible
    snake,
and ends up eating the free sample of the apple
    from the Tree of Knowledge:
thus giving birth to Theology;
or as she opens the tricky gift box containing all
    human evils,

but is stupid enough to believe that Hope will be
    some kind of a solace.

She talks with wolves, without knowing what sort
    of beasts they are:
Where have you been all my life? they ask. *Where have
    I been all my life?* she replies.
We know! *We* know! And we know wolfishness
    when we see it!
Look out, we shout at her silently, thinking of
    all the smart things we would do in her place.
But trapped inside the white pages, she can't hear
    us,
and goes prancing and warbling and lolloping
    innocently towards her doom.
(Innocence! Perhaps that's the key to stupidity,
we tell ourselves, who think we gave it up long ago.)
If she escapes from anything, it's by sheer luck, or
    else the hero:
this girl couldn't tear her way out of a paper bag.

Sometimes she's stupidly fearless; on the other
    · hand,

she can be just as equally fearful, though stupidly
  so.
Incest-minded stepfathers chase her through
  ruined cloisters,
where she's been lured by ruses too transparent to
  fool a gerbil.
Mice make her scream: she whimpers, teeth
  chattering, through the menacing world,
running – but running involves legs, and is grace-
  less – fleeing, rather.
Leglessly she flees, taking the wrong turn at every
  turn,
a white chiffon scarf in the darkness, and we flee
  with her.
Orphaned and minus kind aunts, she makes inap-
  propriate marital choices,
and has to dodge ropes, knives, crazed dogs, stone
  flower-urns toppled off balconies,
aimed at her jittery head by suave, evil husbands
  out for her cash and blood.
Don't feel sorry for her, as she stands there help-
  lessly wringing her hands:
fear is her armour.

Let's face it, she's our inspiration! The Muse as
    fluffball!
And the inspiration of men, as well! Why else were
    the sagas of heroes,
of their godlike strength and superhuman exploits,
    ever composed,
if not for the admiration of women thought stupid
    enough to believe them?
Where did five hundred years of love lyrics come
    from,
not to mention those plaintive imploring songs, all
    musical whines and groans?
Aimed straight at women stupid enough to find
    them seductive!
When lovely woman stoops or bungles her way
    into folly,
pleading her good intentions, her wish to please,
and is taken advantage of, especially by somebody
    famous,
if stupid or smart enough, she gets caught, just as
    in classic novels,
and makes her way into the tabloids, confused and
    tearful,

31

and from there straight into our hearts.
We forgive you! we cry. *We understand! Now do it
some more!*

Hypocrite lecteuse! Ma semblable! Ma soeur!
Let us now praise stupid women,
who have given us Literature.

The Female Body

'. . . *entirely devoted to the subject of "The Female Body."*
Knowing how well you have written on this topic . . . this
capacious topic . . .'
— letter from the *Michigan Quarterly Review*

1

I agree, it's a hot topic. But only one? Look around, there's a wide range. Take my own, for instance.

I get up in the morning. My topic feels like hell. I sprinkle it with water, brush parts of it, rub it with towels, powder it, add lubricant. I dump in the fuel and away goes my topic, my topical topic, my controversial topic, my capacious topic, my limping topic, my nearsighted topic, my topic with back problems, my badly behaved topic, my vulgar topic, my outrageous topic, my ageing topic, my topic that is out of the question and anyway still can't spell, in its oversized coat and worn winter boots, scuttling along the sidewalk as if it were flesh and blood, hunting for what's out there, an avocado, an alderman, an adjective, hungry as ever.

2

The basic Female Body comes with the following accessories: garter-belt, panty-girdle, crinoline, camisole, bustle, brassiere, stomacher, chemise, virgin zone, spike heels, nose-ring, veil, kid gloves, fishnet stockings, fichu, bandeau, Merry Widow, weepers, chokers, barrettes, bangles, beads, lorgnette, feather boa, basic black, compact, Lycra stretch one-piece with modesty panel, designer peignoir, flannel nightie, lace teddy, bed, head.

3

The Female Body is made of transparent plastic and lights up when you plug it in. You press a button to illuminate the different systems. The Circulatory System is red, for the heart and arteries, purple for the veins; the Respiratory System is blue, the Lymphatic System is yellow, the Digestive System is green, with liver and kidneys in aqua. The nerves are done in orange and the brain is pink. The skeleton, as you might expect, is white.

The Reproductive System is optional, and can be removed. It comes with or without a miniature embryo. Parental judgement can thereby be exercised. We do not wish to frighten or offend.

4

He said, I won't have one of those things in the house. It gives a young girl a false notion of beauty, not to

35

mention anatomy. If a real woman was built like that she'd fall on her face.

She said, If we don't let her have one like all the other girls she'll feel singled out. It'll become an issue. She'll long for one and she'll long to turn into one. Repression breeds sublimation. You know that.

He said, It's not just the pointy plastic tits, it's the wardrobes. The wardrobes and that stupid male doll, what's his name, the one with the underwear glued on.

She said, Better to get it over with when she's young. He said, All right but don't let me see it.

She came whizzing down the stairs, thrown like a dart. She was stark naked. Her hair had been chopped off, her head was turned back to front, she was missing some toes and she'd been tattooed all over her body with purple ink, in a scroll-work design. She hit the potted azalea, trembled there for a moment like a botched angel, and fell.

He said, I guess we're safe.

5

The Female Body has many uses. It's been used as a door-knocker, a bottle-opener, as a dock with a ticking belly, as something to hold up lampshades, as a nut-cracker, just squeeze the brass legs together and out comes your nut. It bears torches, lifts victorious wreaths, grows copper wings and raises aloft a ring of neon stars; whole buildings rest on its marble heads.

It sells cars, beer, shaving lotion, cigarettes, hard liquor; it sells diet plans and diamonds, and desire in tiny crystal bottles. Is this the face that launched a thousand products? You bet it is, but don't get any funny big ideas, honey, that smile is a dime a dozen.

It does not merely sell, it is sold. Money flows into this country or that country, flies in, practically crawls in, suitful after suitful, lured by all those hairless pre-teen legs. Listen, you want to reduce the national debt, don't you? Aren't you patriotic? That's the spirit. That's my girl.

She's a natural resource, a renewable one luckily, because those things wear out so quickly. They don't make 'em like they used to. Shoddy goods.

6

One and one equals another one. Pleasure in the female is not a requirement. Pair-bonding is stronger in geese. We're not talking about love, we're talking about biology. That's how we all got here, daughter.

Snails do it differently. They're hermaphrodites, and work in threes.

7

Each female body contains a female brain. Handy. Makes things work. Stick pins in it and you get amazing results. Old popular songs. Short circuits. Bad dreams.

Anyway: each of these brains has two halves. They're

joined together by a thick cord; neural pathways flow from one to the other, sparkles of electric information washing to and fro. Like light on waves. Like a conversation. How does a woman know? She listens. She listens in.

The male brain, now, that's a different matter. Only a thin connection. Space over here, time over there, music and arithmetic in their own sealed compartments. The right brain doesn't know what the left brain is doing. Good for aiming though, for hitting the target when you pull the trigger. What's the target? Who's the target? Who cares? What matters is hitting it. That's the male brain for you. Objective.

This is why men are so sad, why they feel so cut off, why they think of themselves as orphans cast adrift, footloose and stringless in the deep void. What void? she says. What are you talking about? The void of the Universe, he says, and she says Oh and looks out the window and tries to get a handle on it, but it's no use, there's too much going on, too many rustlings in the leaves, too many voices, so she says, Would you like a cheese sandwich, a piece of cake, a cup of tea? And he grinds his teeth because she doesn't understand, and wanders off, not just alone but Alone, lost in the dark, lost in the skull, searching for the other half, the twin who could complete him.

Then it comes to him: he's lost the Female Body! Look, it shines in the gloom, far ahead, a vision of wholeness, ripeness, like a giant melon, like an apple, like a metaphor for *breast* in a bad sex novel; it shines like a balloon, like a foggy noon, a watery moon, shimmering in its egg of light.

Catch it. Put it in a pumpkin, in a high tower, in a compound, in a chamber, in a house, in a room. Quick, stick a leash on it, a lock, a chain, some pain, settle it down, so it can never get away from you again.

In Love With Raymond Chandler

An affair with Raymond Chandler, what a joy! Not because of the mangled bodies and the marinated cops and hints of eccentric sex, but because of his interest in furniture. He knew that furniture could breathe, could feel, not as we do but in a way more muffled, like the word *upholstery*, with its overtones of mustiness and dust, its bouquet of sunlight on ageing cloth or of scuffed leather on the backs and seats of sleazy office chairs. I think of his sofas, stuffed to roundness, satin-covered, pale-blue like the eyes of his cold blonde unbodied murderous women, beating very slowly, like the hearts of hibernating crocodiles; of his chaises longues, with their malicious pillows. He knew about front lawns too, and greenhouses, and the interiors of cars.

This is how our love affair would go. We would meet at a hotel, or a motel, whether expensive or cheap it wouldn't matter. We would enter the room, lock the door, and begin to explore the furniture, fingering the curtains, running our hands along the spurious gilt frames of the pictures, over the real marble or the chipped enamel of the luxurious or tacky washroom sink, inhaling the odour of the carpets, old cigarette smoke and spilled gin and fast meaningless sex or else the rich abstract scent of the oval transparent soaps imported from England, it wouldn't matter to us; what would matter would be our response to the furniture, and the furniture's response to us. Only after we had sniffed, fingered, rubbed, rolled on and absorbed the furniture of the room would we fall into each other's arms, and onto the bed (king-sized? peach-coloured? creaky? narrow? four-posted? pioneer-quilted? lime-green chenille-covered?), ready at last to do the same things to each other.

Stump Hunting

Dead stumps are the favourite disguises of wild animals. How often have you been roaring past in your motor-boat or paddling in your canoe when you've seen a dead stump sticking out of the water and said to yourself, *That looks like an animal?*

Just the head of course. Swimming.

And then when you came up to it, it was only a dead stump.

Don't be deceived! Usually these objects really are animals.

43

Here's what you do.

Shoot the animal, more or less between the eyes, or where you guess the eyes must be. This will kill the animal but will not cause it to shed its disguise.

The next task is getting the animal out of the water. This can be difficult, as the animal will still be holding on tenaciously with the parts of itself that look like roots. You may need a chain-saw, a lot of rope, and a powerful motor on your boat. When you have at last managed to chop and pry the animal loose, tow it to shore, where you will have parked your car.

No blood will be visible.

Let the animal dry out a little. It will be doing a good imitation of being waterlogged and very heavy. Heave it onto the hood of your car or the roof of your van, and rope it down securely. Drive it into the city. Other hunters, with moose or bears or deer or even porcupines strapped to their own cars, will shake their heads and laugh at you, but remember: the last laugh will be yours.

When you get the animal home, butcher it in the backyard. Use the chain-saw again, and a diagram of a cow. The animal will still look like wood. But don't be fooled.

Wrap the steaks, ribs and chops in freezer paper and put them in the freezer. If your wife questions what you are doing or makes disparaging remarks about your sanity, tell her to mind her own business. Conversely, quote from the Bible: *All flesh is grass.*

When you feel ready for a big meal of animal meat, take a steak from the freezer and heat up your charcoal or gas hibachi or your frying-pan or grill. This is the moment at which the animal will be forced to reveal its true nature! Season the steak – we like a little barbecue sauce – and toss it onto the heat.

If it remains wood, you've made a mistake. Bad luck! You've picked the one dead stump out of a thousand that is not really an animal.

Try again later.

2

The favourite disguise of fish is oval stones lying at the bottoms of streams.

Making a Man

This month we'll take a break from crocheted string bikinis and Leftovers Réchaufées to give our readers some tips on how to create, in their very own kitchens and rumpus rooms, an item that is both practical and decorative. It's nice to have one of these around the house, either out on the lawn looking busy, or propped in a chair, prone or erect. Choose the coverings to match the drapes!

When worn out, they can be re-covered and used as doorstops.

1. Traditional Method

Take some dust of the ground. Form. Breathe into the nostrils the breath of life. Simple, but effective!

(Please note that although men are made of dust, women are made of ribs. Remember that at your next Texas-style barbecue!)

Should you give your man a belly button, or not? Authorities on the traditional method disagree. We ourselves like to include one, as we think it adds a finishing touch. Use your thumb.

2. Gingerbread Method

Any good rolled-cookie recipe will do, but add extra ginger if you want lively results; and our readers who choose this method usually do! Raisins make good eyes and buttons, but you can use those little silver balls as long as you take care not to break your teeth on them.

Once your man has come out of your oven, you may have trouble hanging on to him. Men made this way are apt to take off down the road, on motorcycles or off them, robbing convenience stores, getting themselves tattooed, and hopping up and down and singing, 'Run, run, as fast as you can, you can't catch me, I'm the Gingerbread Man!' Attaching a string to his leg before the oven procedure may help, but – alas – in our experience, not for long.

There's one good thing to be said for this method, though: these guys are scrumptious! Good enough to eat!

3. Clothes Method

Clothes make the man! How often have you heard it said!

Well, we couldn't agree more! However, clothes may make the man, but women – by and large – make the clothes, so it follows that the responsibility for the finished model lies with the home seamstress.

Use a good pattern and cut on the lines. Otherwise your man will be all screw-jiggy. Pre-shrink the fabric, or your man will turn out to be smaller than you'd hoped. Sew the darts first, and remember to give that tummy a good tuck, or you'll be sorry later! Watch those zippers. A badly placed zipper can cause serious functional problems. It's fun to be different, but not too different!

Casual or formal is up to you; if in doubt, make two, and alternate. Be sure your house has a lot of mirrors. Men made this way – like budgies – seem to adore them!

One very creative woman we know sewed her entire man out of rubber sheeting. Then she used a bicycle pump. Amazing!

4. Marzipan Method

We've often thought men would be easier to control if they were smaller. Well, here's a tiny rascal you can hold in the palm of your hand!

Usually found on wedding cakes, these formally dressed mini-grooms require painstaking attention to detail, but it's worth the time you spend with the paintbrush and the food colouring to see the finished result smiling at you with deceptive blandness from the frothy topmost layer of Seven-Minute Boiled Icing!

We much regret the modern custom of substituting plastic for the original sugary confection. For one thing, there is absolutely no payoff when you feel the urge – as we do! – to pop one of these dapper devils into your mouth and suck off his clothes.

5. Folk Art Method

You've seen these cuties in other folks' front yards, with little windmills attached to their heads. They hammer with their little hammers, saw with their little saws, or just whirl their arms around a lot when there's a stiff breeze. Alternatively, they may just stand stock-still, holding onto bridles, lanterns or fishing poles. Some of them may be in gnome costumes.

Why shouldn't you concoct one of these cunning fellows for your very own? No reason at all! Just coat your hubby with plaster of Paris, and

Epaulettes

When war had finally become too dangerous, and, more to the point, too expensive for everyone, the world leaders met informally to devise a substitute.

'The thing is,' said the first speaker, 'what purposes did war serve when we had it?'

'It stimulated production in selected areas of the economy,' said one.

'It provided clear winners and clear losers,' said another, 'and it gave men a break from the boring and trivial domestic routine.'

'Expansion of territory,' said another. 'Privileged access to females and other items in demand.'

'It was exciting,' said a fourth. 'Something was at risk.'

'Well then,' said the first, 'these are the benefits our substitute for war must provide.'

At first the world leaders focused their attention on sports, and a lively discussion ensued. Baseball, basketball, and cricket were dismissed as too leisurely. Football and hockey were both seriously proposed, until it became evident that no world leader would last two minutes on either Astroturf or ice. One of the world leaders, who was interested in archaeology, suggested an old Mayan game played in sunken ball-courts, in which the loser's head was ceremonially cut off, but the rules of this game were no longer known.

'We are looking in the wrong area,' said a world leader from one of the smaller countries. 'Forget these rowdy games. We should be thinking birds.'

'Birds?' said the others, sneering both politely – in the case of the older and more machiavellian nations and less politely, in the case of the younger and cruder ones.

'Bird display,' said the speaker. 'The male birds, in their elaborate and brightly coloured plumage, strut about, sing, ruffle their feathers, and perform dances. The watching female birds choose the winners. This is a simple and I might add a melodious method of competition, and has much to recommend it. Let me just add, gentlemen, that it has worked for the birds.'

The great powers were against this proposal, as it would pit their own leaders against those of the smaller nations on a more or less equal footing. But for this same reason the smaller nations were in favour of it, and because there were more of them than there were of the great powers, the resolution was voted in.

_____

Which leads to the happy state of affairs we enjoy today. Once a year, in April, the play-offs begin. Throngs of chattering and expectant women crowd the football, cricket and jai alai stadia of the world. Each is provided with a voting device, with pushbuttons ranging from 0 to 10. The world leaders compete in groups of six, with the winner going on to the next round until, finally, there is only one winner for the entire world.

During the subsequent year the men of the winning country enjoy certain privileges, which include: modified looting (department stores only, and only on Mondays); ordering loudly and banging the tables in restaurants; having the men from all other nations laugh at their witticisms in a grovelling manner; preferential dating; complimentary theatre tickets; and two days of rape and pillage, followed by ritual drunkenness in the streets. (As everyone knows which days are the two chosen ones, people simply board up their windows and go away for the weekend.) Winners also get an improved foreign exchange rate and the best deals on fish processing. Each country enjoys its triumphant status for a year only, and since all know that next year it will be somebody else's turn – the women see to that – the more extreme forms of riotous behaviour are self-policed.

The competition itself is divided into several categories. Each one of these is designed to appeal to the female temperament, though there has been some difficulty in determining exactly what this is. For instance, the 'aroma' category – in which the condensed essences of the competitors' sweat-socks, cigars, used tennis shirts, and so forth, were wafted through the audience – had to be discontinued, as it made too many women sick. But the name-calling, muscle-flexing and cool-dressing bouts remain. So does joke-telling, since it is well known that women prefer men with a sense of humour, or so they keep telling us. In addition, a song must be sung, a dance must be danced – though a solo on the flute or cello will suffice – a skill-testing question must be answered; and each world leader must describe his favourite hobby, and declare, in a well-modulated exhibition speech, what he intends to do in future for the good of humanity. This is a popular feature, and occasions much giggling and applause.

Best of all is the military uniform category, during which the contestants march along the runway to the sound of recorded brass bands. What colours we see then, what festoons of gold braid, what constellations of metal stars! Gone are the days of muted khaki, even of navy blue: we live in the age of the peacock. Epaulettes have swollen to epic lengths and breadths, headgear is befeathered, beribboned, resplendent! The stimulus to the fashion industry has been prodigious.

From our new system a new type of world leader has emerged. Younger, for one thing. Lighter on the feet. More musical. Funnier.

And history too is being revised. Daring military exploits, megadeaths, genocides and other such emblems of conquistadorial prowess no longer count for much. The criteria have changed. It is being said, for instance, that Napoleon was practically a catatonic on the dance floor, and that Stalin wore ill-fitting uniforms and could not sing to save his life.

Cold-Blooded

To my sisters, the Iridescent Ones, the Egg-Bearers, the Many-Faceted, greetings from the Planet of Moths.

At last we have succeeded in establishing contact with the creatures here who, in their ability to communicate, to live in colonies and to construct technologies, most resemble us, although in these particulars they have not advanced above a rudimentary level.

During our first observation of these 'blood-creatures,' as we have termed them – after the colourful red liquid which is to be found inside their bodies, and which appears to be of great significance to them in their poems, wars and religious rituals – we supposed them incapable of speech, as those specimens we were able to examine entirely lacked the organs for it. They had no wing-casings with which to stribulate – indeed they had no wings; they had no mandibles to click; and the chemical method was unknown to them, since they were devoid of antennae. 'Smell,' for them, is a perfunctory affair, confined to a flattened and numbed appendage on the front of the head. But after a time, we discovered that the incoherent squeakings and gruntings that emerged from them, especially when pinched, were in fact a form of language, and after that we made rapid progress.

We soon ascertained that their planet, named by us the Planet of Moths after its most prolific and noteworthy genus, is called by these creatures *Earth*. They have some notion that their ancestors were created from this substance; or so it is claimed in many of their charming but irrational folk-tales.

In an attempt to establish common ground, we asked them at what season they mated with and then devoured their males. Imagine our embarrassment when we discovered that those individuals with whom we were conversing *were* males! (It is very hard to tell the difference, as their males are not diminutive, as ours are, but if anything bigger. Also, lacking natural beauty – brilliantly patterned carapaces, diaphanous wings, luminescent eyes, and the like – they attempt to imitate our kind by placing upon their bodies various multicoloured draperies, which conceal their generative parts.)

We apologized for our faux pas, and enquired as to their own sexual practices. Picture our nausea and disgust when we discovered that it is the male, not the egg-bearer, which is the most prized among them! Abnormal as this will seem to you, my sisters, their leaders are for the most part male; which may account for their state of relative barbarism. Another peculiarity which must be noted is that, although they frequently kill them in many other ways, they rarely devour their females after pro-creation. This is a waste of protein; but then, they are a wasteful people.

We hastily abandoned this painful subject.

Next we asked them when they pupated. Here again, as in the case of 'clothing' – the draperies we have men-tioned – we uncovered a fumbling attempt at imitation of our kind. At some indeterminate point in their life cycles, they cause themselves to be placed in artificial stone or wooden cocoons, or chrysalises. They have an idea that they will someday emerge from these in an altered state, which they symbolize with carvings of themselves with wings. However, we did not observe that any had actually done so.

It is as well to mention at this juncture that, in addition to the many species of moths for which it is justly famous among us, the Planet of Moths abounds in thousands of varieties of creatures which resemble our own distant ancestors. It seems that one of our previous attempts at colonization – an attempt so distant that our record of it is lost – must have borne fruit. However, these beings, although numerous and ingenious, are small in size and primitive in their social organization, and attempts to communicate with them were not – or have not been, so far – very successful. The blood-creatures are hostile towards them, and employ against them many poisonous sprays, traps and so forth, in addition to a sinister manual device termed a 'fly swatter.' It is agonizing indeed to watch one of these instruments of torture and death being wielded by the large and frenzied against the small and helpless; but the rules of diplomacy forbid our intervention. (Luckily the blood-creatures cannot understand what we say to one another about them in our own language.)

But despite all the machinery of destruction which is

aimed at them, our distant relatives are more than holding their own. They feed on the crops and herd-animals
and even on the flesh of the blood-creatures; they live in
their homes, devour their clothes, hide and flourish in
the very cracks of their floors. When the blood-creatures
have succeeded at last in overbreeding themselves, as it
seems their intention to do, or in exterminating one
another, rest assured that our kind, already superior in
both numbers and adaptability, will be poised to achieve
the ascendency which is ours by natural right.

This will not happen tomorrow, but it will happen. As
you know, my sisters, we have long been a patient race.

Men at Sea

You can come to the end of talking, about women, talking. In restaurants, cafés, kitchens, less frequently in bars or pubs, about relatives, relations, relationships, illnesses, jobs, children, men; about nuance, hunch, intimation, intuition, shadow; about themselves and each other; about what he said to her and she said to her and she said back; about what they feel.

Something more definite, more outward then, some action, to drain the inner swamp, sweep the inner fluff out from under the inner bed, harden the edges. Men at sea, for instance. Not on a submarine, too claustrophobic and smelly, but something more bracing, a tang of salt, cold water, all over your calloused body, cuts and bruises, hurricanes, bravery and above all no women. Women are replaced by water, by wind, by the ocean, shifting and treacherous; a man has to know what to do, to navigate, to sail, to bail, so reach for the How-To book, and out here it's what he said to him, or didn't say, a narrowing of the eyes, sizing the bastard up before the pounce, the knife to the gut, and here comes a wave, hang on to the shrouds, all teeth grit, all muscles bulge together. Or sneaking along the gangway, the passageway, the right of way, the Milky Way, in the dark, your eyes shining like digital wrist-watches, and the bushes, barrels, scuppers, ditches, filthy with enemies, and you on the prowl for adrenalin and loot. Corpses of your own making deliquesce behind you as you reach the cave, abandoned city, safe, sliding panel, hole in the ground, and rich beyond your wildest dreams!

What now? Spend it on some woman, in a restaurant. And there I am, back again at the eternal table, which exists so she can put her elbows on it, over a glass of wine, while he says. What does he say? He says the story of how he got here, to her. She says: But what did you feel?

And his eyes roll wildly, quick as a wink he tries to think of something else, a cactus, a porpoise, never give yourself away, while the seductive waves swell the carpet beneath the feet and the wind freshens among the table-cloths. They're all around her, she can see it now, one per woman per table. Men, at sea.

Alien Territory

1

He conceives himself in alien territory. Not his turf —
alien! Listen! The rushing of the red rivers, the rustling of
the fresh leaves in the dusk, always in the dusk, under the
dark stars, and the wish-wash, wish-wash of the heavy
soothing sea, which becomes — yes! — the drums of the
natives, beating, beating, louder, faster, lower, slower. Are
they hostile? Who knows, because they're invisible.

He sleeps and wakes, wakes and sleeps, and suddenly all
is movement and suffering and terror and he is shot out
gasping for breath into blinding light and a place that's
even more dangerous, where food is scarce and two enormous giants stand guard over his wooden prison. Shout

as he might, rattle the bars, nobody comes to let him out. One of the giants is boisterous and hair-covered, with a big stick; the other walks more softly but has two enormous bulgy comforts which she selfishly refuses to detach and give away, to him. Neither of them looks anything like him, and their language is incomprehensible.

Aliens! What can he do? And to make it worse, they surround him with animals bears, rabbits, cats, giraffes each one of them stuffed and, evidently, castrated, because although he looks and looks, all they have at best is a tail. Is this the fate the aliens have in store for him, as well?

Where did I come from? he asks, for what will not be the first time. *Out of me*, the bulgy one says fondly, as if he should be pleased. Out of *where*? Out of *what*? He covers his ears, shutting out the untruth, the shame, the pulpy horror. It is not to be thought, it is not to be borne!

No wonder that at the first opportunity he climbs out the window and joins a gang of other explorers, each one of them an exile, an immigrant, like himself. Together they set out on their solitary journeys.

What are they searching for? Their homeland. Their true country. The place they came from, which can't possibly be here.

2

All men are created equal, as someone said who was either very hopeful or very mischievous. What a lot of anxiety could have been avoided if he'd only kept his mouth shut.

Sigmund was wrong about the primal scene: Mom and Dad, keyhole version. That might be upsetting, true, but there's another one:

Five guys standing outside, pissing into a snowbank, a river, the underbrush, pretending not to look down. Or maybe *not* looking down: gazing upward, at the stars, which gives us the origin of astronomy.

Anything to avoid comparisons, which aren't so much odious as intimidating.

And not only astronomy: quantum physics, engineering, laser technology, all numeration between zero and infinity. Something safely abstract, detached from you; a transfer of the obsession with size to anything at all. Lord, Lord, they measure everything: the height of the Great Pyramids, the rate of fingernail growth, the multiplication of viruses, the sands of the sea, the number of angels that can dance on the head of a pin. And then it's only a short step to proving that God is a mathematical equation. Not a person. Not a body, Heaven forbid. Not one like yours. Not an earthbound one, not one with size and therefore pain.

When you're feeling blue, just keep on whistling. Just keep on measuring. Just don't look down.

3

The history of war is a history of killed bodies. That's what war is: bodies killing other bodies, bodies being killed.

Some of the killed bodies are those of women and children, as a side-effect you might say. Fallout, shrapnel, napalm, rape and skewering, anti-personnel devices. But most of the killed bodies are men. So are most of those doing the killing.

Why do men want to kill the bodies of other men? Women don't want to kill the bodies of other women. By and large. As far as we know.

Here are some traditional reasons: Loot. Territory. Lust for power. Hormones. Adrenalin high. Rage. God. Flag. Honour. Righteous anger. Revenge. Oppression. Slavery. Starvation. Defence of one's life. Love; or, a desire to protect the women and children. From what? From the bodies of other men.

What men are most afraid of is not lions, not snakes, not the dark, not women. Not any more. What men are most afraid of is the body of another man.

Men's bodies are the most dangerous things on earth.

4

On the other hand, it could be argued that men don't have any bodies at all. Look at the magazines! Magazines for women have women's bodies on the covers, magazines for men have women's bodies on the covers. When men appear on the covers of magazines, it's magazines about money, or about world news. Invasions, rocket launches, political coups, interest rates, elections, medical breakthroughs. *Reality*. Not *entertainment*. Such magazines show only the heads, the unsmiling heads, the talking heads, the decision-making heads, and maybe a little glimpse, a coy flash of suit. How do we know there's a body, under all that discreet pinstriped tailoring? We don't, and maybe there isn't.

What does this lead us to suppose? That women are bodies with heads attached, and men are heads with bodies attached? Or not, depending.

You can have a body, though, if you're a rock star, an

athlete, or a gay model. As I said, *entertainment*. Having a body is not altogether serious.

5

The thing is: men's bodies aren't dependable. Now it does, now it doesn't, and so much for the triumph of the will. A man is the puppet of his body, or vice versa. He and it make tomfools of each other: it lets him down. Or up, at the wrong moment. Just stare hard out the schoolroom window and recite the multiplication tables, and pretend this isn't happening! Your face at least can be immobile. Easier to have a trained dog, which will do what you want it to, nine times out of ten.

The other thing is: men's bodies are detachable. Consider the history of statuary: the definitive bits get knocked off so easily, through revolution or prudery or simple transportation, with leaves stuck on for substitutes, fig or grape; or, in more northern climates, maple. A man and his body are soon parted.

In the old old days, you became a man through blood. Through incisions, tattoos, splinters of wood; through an intimate wound, and the refusal to flinch. Through being beaten by older boys, in the dormitory, with a wooden paddle you were forced to carve yourself. The torments varied, but they were all torments. *It's a boy*, they cry with joy. *Let's cut some off!*

Every morning I get down on my knees and thank God for not creating me a man. A man so chained to unpredictability. A man so much at the mercy of himself. A man so prone to sadness. A man who has to take it like a man. A man, who can't fake it.

In the gap between desire and enactment, noun and verb, intention and infliction, *want* and *have*, compassion begins.

6

Bluebeard ran off with the third sister, intelligent though beautiful, and shut her up in his palace. *Everything here is yours, my dear*, he said to her. *Just don't open the small door. I will give you the key, however. I expect you not to use it.*

Believe it or not, this sister was in love with him, even though she knew he was a serial killer. She roamed over the whole palace, ignoring the jewels and the silk dresses and the piles of gold. Instead she went through the medicine cabinet and the kitchen drawers, looking for clues to his uniqueness. Because she loved him, she wanted to understand him. She also wanted to cure him. She thought she had the healing touch.

But she didn't find out a lot. In his closet there were suits and ties and matching shoes and casual wear, some golf outfits and a tennis racquet, and some jeans for when he wanted to rake up the leaves. Nothing unusual, nothing kinky, nothing sinister. She had to admit to being a little disappointed.

She found his previous women quite easily. They were in the linen closet, neatly cut up and ironed flat and folded, stored in mothballs and lavender. Bachelors acquire such domestic skills. The women didn't make much of an impression on her, except the one who looked like his mother. That one she took out with rubber gloves on and slipped into the incinerator in the garden. *Maybe it was his mother*, she thought. *If so, good riddance*.

She read through his large collection of cookbooks, and prepared the dishes on the most-thumbed pages. At dinner he was politeness itself, pulling out her chair and offering more wine and leading the conversation around to topics of the day. She said gently that she wished he would talk more about his feelings. He said that if she had his feelings, she wouldn't want to talk about them either. This intrigued her. She was now more in love with him and more curious than ever.

Well, she thought, *I've tried everything else; it's the small door or nothing. Anyway, he gave me the key*. She waited until he had gone to the office or wherever it was he went, and made straight for the small door. When she opened it, what should be inside but a dead child. A small dead child, with its eyes wide open.

It's mine, he said, coming up behind her. *I gave birth to it. I warned you. Weren't you happy with me?*

It looks like you, she said, not turning around, not knowing what else to say. She realized now that he was not sane in any known sense of the word, but she still hoped to talk her way out of it. She could feel the love seeping out of her. Her heart was dry ice.

It is me, he said sadly. *Don't be afraid.*

Where are we going? she said, because it was getting dark, and there was suddenly no floor.

Deeper, he said.

7

Those ones. Why do women like them? They have nothing to offer, none of the usual things. They have short attention spans, falling-apart clothes, old beat-up cars, if any. The cars break down, and they try to fix them, and don't succeed, and give up. They go on long walks from which they forget to return. They prefer weeds to flowers. They tell trivial fibs. They perform clumsy tricks with oranges and pieces of string, hoping desperately that someone will laugh. They don't put food on the table. They don't make money. Don't, can't, won't.

They offer nothing. They offer the great clean sweep of nothing, the unseen sky during a blizzard, the dark pause between moon and moon. They offer their poverty, an empty wooden bowl; the bowl of a beggar, whose gift is to ask. Look into it, look down deep, where potential coils like smoke, and you might hear anything. Nothing has yet been said.

They have bodies, however. Their bodies are unlike the bodies of other men. Their bodies are verbalized. *Mouth, eye, hand, foot,* they say. Their bodies have weight, and move over the ground, step by step, like yours. Like you they roll in the hot mud of the sunlight, like you they are amazed by morning, like you they can taste the wind, like you they sing. *Love,* they say, and at the time they always mean it, as you do also. They can say *lust* as well, and *disgust*; you wouldn't trust them otherwise. They say the worst things you have ever dreamed. They open locked doors. All this is given to them for nothing.

They have their angers. They have their despair, which washes over them like grey ink, blanking them out, leaving them immobile, in metal kitchen chairs, beside closed windows, looking out at the brick walls of deserted factories, for years and years. Yet nothing is with them; it keeps faith with them, and from it they bring back messages:

Hurt, they say, and suddenly their bodies hurt again, like real bodies. *Death*, they say, making the word sound like the backwash of a wave. Their bodies die, and waver, and turn to mist. And yet they can exist in two worlds at once: lost in the earth or eaten by flames, and here. In this room, when you re-say them, in their own words.

But why do women like them? Not *like*, I mean to say: *adore*. (Remember, that despite everything, despite all I have told you, the rusted cars, the greasy wardrobes, the lack of breakfasts, the hopelessness, remain the same.)

Because if they can say their own bodies, they could say yours also. Because they could say *skin* as if it meant something, not only to them but to you. Because one night, when the snow is falling and the moon is blotted out, they could put their empty hands, their hands filled with poverty, their beggar's hands, on your body, and bless it, and tell you it is made of light.

Adventure Story

This is a story told by our ancestors, and those before them. It is not just a story, but something they once did, and at last there is proof.

Those who are to go must prepare first. They must be strong and well nourished and they must possess also a sense of purpose, a faith, a determination to persevere to the end, because the way is long and arduous and there are many dangers.

At the right time they gather together in the appointed place. Here there is much confusion and milling around, as yet there is no order, no groups of sworn companions have separated themselves from the rest. The atmosphere is tense, anticipation stirs among them, and now, before some are ready, the adventure has been launched. Through the dark tunnel, faintly lit with lurid gleams of reddish light, shoots the intrepid band, how many I cannot say; only that there are many: a band now, for all are headed in the same direction. The safety of the home country falls behind, the sea between is crossed more quickly than you can think, and now they are in alien territory, a tropical estuary with many coves and hidden bays. The water is salt, the vegetation Amazonian, the land ahead shrouded and obscure, thickened with fog. Monstrous animals, or are they fish, lurk here, pouncing upon the stragglers, slaying many. Others are lost, and wander until they weaken and perish in misery.

Now the way narrows, and those who have survived have reached the gate. It is shut, but they try one password and then another, and look! the gate has softened, melted, turned to jelly, and they pass through. Magic still works; an unseen force is on their side. Another tunnel; here they must crowd together, swimming upstream, between shores curving and fluid as lava, helping one another. Only together can they succeed.

(You may think I'm talking about male bonding, or war, but no: half of these are female, and they swim and help and sacrifice their lives in the same way as the rest.)

And now there is a widening out, and the night

sky arches above them, or are we in outer space and all the rocket movies you've ever seen? It's still warm, whatever, and the team, its number sadly diminished, forges onward, driven by what? Greed for treasure, desire for a new home, worlds to conquer, a raid on an enemy citadel, a quest for the Grail? Now it is each alone, and the mission becomes a race which only one may win, as, ahead of them, vast and luminous, the longed-for, the loved planet swims into view, like a moon, a sun, an image of God, round and perfect. A target.

Farewell, my comrades, my sisters! You have died that I may live! I alone will enter the garden, while you must wilt and shrivel in outer darkness. So saying – and you know, because now this is less like a story than a memory – the victorious one reaches the immense perimeter and is engulfed in the soft pink atmosphere of paradise, sinks, enters, casts the imprisoning skin of the self, merges, disappears ... and the world slowly explodes, doubles, revolves, changes forever, and there, in the desert heaven, shines a fresh-laid star, exile and promised land in one, harbinger of a new order, a new birth, possibly holy; and the animals will be named again.

Hardball

Here comes the future, rolling towards us like a meteorite, a satellite, a giant iron snowball, a two-ton truck in the wrong lane, careering downhill with broken brakes, and whose fault is it? No time to think about that. Blink and it's here.

How round, how firm, how fully packed is this future! How man-made! What wonders it contains, especially for those who can afford it! They are the elect, and by their fruits ye shall know them. Their fruits are strawberries and dwarf plums and grapes, things that can be grown beside the hydroponic vegetables and the toxin-absorbent ornamentals, in relatively little space. Space is at a premium, living space that is. All space that is not living space is considered dead.

Living space is under the stately pleasure dome, the

work-and-leisure dome, the transparent bubble-dome that keeps out the deadly cosmic rays and the rain of sulphuric acid and the air which is no longer. No longer air, I mean. You can look out, of course: watch the sun, red at all times of day, rise across the raw rock and shifting sands, travel across the raw rock and shifting sands, set across the raw rock and shifting sands. The light effects are something.

But breathing is out of the question. That's a thing you have to do in here, and the richer you are the better you do it. Penthouse costs a bundle; steerage is cramped, and believe me it stinks. Well, as they say, there's only so much to go around, and it wouldn't do if everyone got the same. No incentive then, to perform the necessary work, make the necessary sacrifices, inch your way up, to where the pale-pink strawberries and the pale-yellow carrots are believed, still, to grow.

What else is eaten? Well, there are no more hamburgers. Cows take up too much room. Chickens and rabbits are still cultivated, here and there; they breed quickly and they're small. Rats, of course, on the lower levels, if you can catch them. Think of the earth as an eighteenth-century ship, with stowaways but no destination.

And no fish, needless to say. None left in all that dirty water sloshing around in the oceans and through the remains of what used to be New York. If you're really loaded you can go diving there, for your vacation. Travel by airlock. Plunge into the romance of a bygone age. But it's an ill wind that blows nobody any good. No more street crime. Think of it as a plus.

Back to the topic of food, which will always be of interest. What will we have for dinner? Is it wall-to-wall bean sprouts? Apart from the pallid garnishes and the chicken-hearted hors-d'oeuvres, what's the main protein?

Think of the earth as a nineteenth-century lifeboat, adrift in the open sea, with castaways but no rescuers. After a while you run out of food, you run out of water. You run out of everything but your fellow passengers.

Why be squeamish? Let's just say we've learned the hard way about waste. Or let's say we all make our little contribution to the general welfare, in the end.

It's done by computer. For every birth there must be a death. Everything's ground up, naturally. Nothing you might recognize, such as fingers. Think of the earth as a hard stone ball, scraped clean of life. There are benefits: no more mosquitoes, no bird poop on your car. The bright side is a survival tool. So look on it.

I'm being unnecessarily brutal, you say. Too blunt, too graphic. You want things to go on the way they are, five square meals a day, new plastic toys, the wheels of the economy oiled and spinning, payday as usual, the smoke going up the chimney just the same. You don't like this future.

You don't like this future? Switch it off. Order another. Return to sender.

My Life as a Bat

1. Reincarnation

In my previous life I was a bat.

If you find previous lives amusing or unlikely, you are not a serious person. Consider: a great many people believe in them, and if sanity is a general consensus about the content of reality, who are you to disagree?

Consider also: previous lives have entered the world of commerce. Money can be made from them. *You were Cleopatra, you were a Flemish Duke, you were a Druid priestess*, and money changes hands. If the stock market exists, so must previous lives.

In the previous-life market, there is not such a great demand for Peruvian ditch-diggers as there is for Cleopatra; or for Indian latrine-cleaners, or for 1952 housewives living in California split-levels. Similarly, not many of us choose to remember our lives as vultures, spiders or rodents, but some of us do. The fortunate few. Conventional wisdom has it that reincarnation as an animal is a punishment for past sins, but perhaps it is a reward instead. At least a resting place. An interlude of grace.

Bats have a few things to put up with, but they do not inflict. When they kill, they kill without mercy, but without hate. They are immune from the curse of pity. They never gloat.

2. Nightmares

I have recurring nightmares.

In one of them, I am clinging to the ceiling of a summer cottage while a red-faced man in white shorts and a white V-necked T-shirt jumps up and down, hitting at me with a tennis racquet. There are cedar rafters up here, and sticky flypapers attached with tacks, dangling like toxic seaweeds. I look down at the man's face, foreshortened and sweating, the eyes bulging and blue, the mouth emitting furious noise, rising up like a marine float, sinking again, rising as if on a swell of air.

The air itself is muggy, the sun is sinking; there will be a thunderstorm. A woman is shrieking, 'My hair! My hair!' and someone else is calling, 'Anthea! Bring the stepladder!' All I want is to get out through the hole in the screen, but that will take some concentration and it's hard in this din of voices, they interfere with my sonar. There is a smell of dirty bath-mats – it's his breath, the breath that comes out from every pore, the breath of the monster. I will be lucky to get out of this alive.

In another nightmare I am winging my way – flittering, I suppose you'd call it – through the clean-washed demi-light before dawn. This is a desert. The yuccas are in bloom, and I have been gorging myself on their juices and pollen. I'm heading to my home, to my home cave, where it will be cool during the burnout of day and there will be the sound of water trickling through limestone, coating the rock with a glistening hush, with the moistness of new mushrooms, and the other bats will chirp and rustle and doze until night unfurls again and makes the hot sky tender for us.

But when I reach the entrance to the cave, it is sealed over. It's blocked in. Who can have done this?

I vibrate my wings, sniffing blind as a dazzled moth over the hard surface. In a short time the sun will rise like a balloon on fire and I will be blasted with its glare, shrivelled to a few small bones.

Whoever said that light was life and darkness nothing?

For some of us, the mythologies are different.

3. Vampire Films

I became aware of the nature of my previous life gradually, not only through dreams but through scraps of memory, through hints, through odd moments of recognition.

There was my preference for the subtleties of dawn and dusk, as opposed to the vulgar blaring hour of high noon. There was my déjà vu experience in the Carlsbad Caverns – surely I had been there before, long before, before they put in the pastel spotlights and the cute names for stalactites and the underground restaurant where you can combine claustrophobia and indigestion and then take the elevator to get back out.

There was also my dislike for headfuls of human hair, so like nets or the tendrils of poisonous jellyfish: I feared entanglements. No real bat would ever suck the blood of necks. The neck is too near the hair. Even the vampire bat will target a hairless extremity: by choice a toe, resembling as it does the teat of a cow.

Vampire films have always seemed ludicrous to me, for this reason but also for the idiocy of their bats – huge rubbery bats, with red Christmas-light eyes and fangs like a sabre-toothed tiger's, flown in on strings, their puppet wings flapped sluggishly like those of an over-weight and degenerate bird. I screamed at these filmic moments, but not with fear; rather with outraged laughter, at the insult to bats.

O Dracula, unlikely hero! O flying leukemia, in your cloak like a living umbrella, a membrane of black leather which you unwind from within yourself and lift like a stripteaser's fan as you bend with emaciated lust over the neck, flawless and bland, of whatever woman is longing for obliteration, here and now in her best negligee. Why was it given to you by whoever stole your soul to transform yourself into bat and wolf, and only those? Why not a vampire chipmunk, a duck, a gerbil? Why not a vampire turtle? Now that would be a plot.

4. The Bat as a Deadly Weapon

During the Second World War they did experiments with bats. Thousands of bats were to be released over German cities, at the hour of noon. Each was to have a small incendiary device strapped onto it, with a timer. The bats would have headed for darkness, as is their habit. They would have crawled into holes in walls, or secreted themselves under the eaves of houses, relieved to have found safety. At a preordained moment they would have exploded, and the cities would have gone up in flames.

That was the plan. Death by flaming bat. The bats too would have died, of course. Acceptable megadeaths.

The cities went up in flames anyway, but not with the aid of bats. The atom bomb had been invented, and the fiery bat was no longer thought necessary.

If the bats had been used after all, would there have been a war memorial to them? It isn't likely.

If you ask a human being what makes his flesh creep more, a bat or a bomb, he will say the bat. It is difficult to experience loathing for something merely metal, however ominous. We save these sensations for those with skin and flesh: a skin, a flesh, unlike our own.

5. Beauty

Perhaps it isn't my life as a bat that was the interlude. Perhaps it is this life. Perhaps I have been sent into human form as if on a dangerous mission, to save and redeem my own folk. When I have gained a small success, or died in the attempt – for failure, in such a task and against such odds, is more likely – I will be born again, back into that other form, that other world where I truly belong.

More and more, I think of this event with longing. The quickness of heartbeat, the vivid plunge into the nectars of crepuscular flowers, hovering in the infrared of night; the dank lazy half-sleep of daytime, with bodies rounded and soft as furred plums clustering around me, the mothers licking the tiny amazed faces of the newborn; the swift love of what will come next, the anticipations of the tongue and of the infurled, corrugated and scrolled nose, nose like a dead leaf, nose like a radiator grill, nose of a denizen of Pluto.

And in the evening, the supersonic hymn of praise to our Creator, the Creator of bats, who appears to us in the form of a bat and who gave us all things: water and the liquid stone of caves, the woody refuge of attics, petals and fruit and juicy insects, and the beauty of slippery wings and sharp white canines and shining eyes.

What do we pray for? We pray for food as all do, and for health and for the increase of our kind; and for deliverance from evil, which cannot be explained by us, which is hair-headed and walks in the night with a single white unseeing eye, and stinks of half-digested meat, and has two legs.

Goddess of caves and grottoes: bless your children.

Theology

At school we prayed a lot. There was nothing to it. Every morning in the home-room, a little scriptural reading, too, and more in assemblies, the principal pious over the P.A. system, the auditorium light-green like a hospital, whispering and shuffling among the rows of quite-new seats, and after the prayer the daily exhortation to pick up your gum wrappers. This was in the age of ducktails; there was a lot of gum around.

Once the Latin teacher said in a horrified voice: Don't put the attendance slip *there*! Not on top of the *Bible*!

Here is what I would think about during the prayers, and sometimes in Latin class, too. If Heaven is a good place and preferable to earth, why is murdering good people bad? Wouldn't you be doing them a favour, since that way they'd get up there sooner? Only murdering bad people should be bad, since they weren't about to go to Heaven anyway. But if they were bad enough, surely they deserved to be murdered. So murdering both good people and bad people was actually quite good, all things considered: to the good people you'd be giving a helping hand, to the bad ones their just deserts.

I told some of this to my friend S., on the way home from school, past the Bayview movie theatre with its ceiling pocked with spitballs, past Kresge's with its dim lighting and wooden floors and brooches made from dyed feathers and gilt picture-frames containing, for display purposes, murkily coloured photographs of movie stars from ten years before; where, it was rumoured, you would end up working if you flunked your year or slipped up badly in a back seat. We wore pencil skirts then, shortie coats, velveteen ballerina-shoes that caved out at the arches after a few wearings.

What interested me was the thought of all those righteous murders, and the people who would do them. I had my ideas about that; even among the high-school teachers you could tell who wouldn't, who would enjoy it, who would say it was all for the best. Religion, it seemed to me, could get out of hand.

My friend S. went to the Unitarians, who sang badly but had kind ideas. At Christmas her family did their tree in a theme, all blue gauze or all silver balls, not haphazard like the rest of us.

S. thought about the murder theory, but not for long. She did not think I was being serious.

God is the good in people, she would say, from time to time.

Like vitamins in milk? I'd ask. So if everyone died that would be the end of God?

No, she would say. I don't know. I need a cigarette. Don't make me dizzy.

My friend S. went to the Unitarians, who sang badly but had kind ideas. At Christmas her family did their tree in a theme, all blue gauze or all silver balls, not baptize-and like the rest of us.

So thought about the murder theory, but not for long.

She did not think I was being serious.

God is the good in people, she would say, from time to time.

Like vitamins in milk? I'd ask. So if everyone died that would be the end of God?

No, she would say, I don't know. I need a cigarette. Don't make me dizzy.

An Angel

I know what the angel of suicide looks like. I have seen her several times. She's around.

She's nothing like the pictures of angels you run across here and there, the ones in classical paintings, with their curls and beautiful eyelashes, or the ones on Christmas cards, all cute or white. Much is made, in these pictures, of the feet, which are always bare, I suppose to show that angels do not need shoes: walkers on nails and live coals all of them, aspirin hearts, dandelion-seed heads, air bodies.

Not so the angel of suicide, who is dense, heavy with antimatter, a dark star. But despite the differences, she does have something in common with those others. All angels are messengers, and so is she; which isn't to say that all messages are good. The angels vary according to what they have to say: the angel of blindness for instance, the angel of lung cancer, the angel of seizures, the destroying angel. The latter is also a mushroom.

(Snow angels, you've seen them: the cold blank shape of yourself, the outline you once filled. They too are messengers, they come from the future. This is what you will be, they say; perhaps what you are: no more than the way light falls across a given space.)

Angels come in two kinds: the others, and those who fell. The angel of suicide is one of those who fell, down through the atmosphere to the earth's surface. Or did she jump? With her you have to ask.

Anyway, it was a long fall. From the friction of the air, her face melted off like the skin of a meteor. That is why the angel of suicide is so smooth. She has no face to speak of. She has the face of a grey egg. Non-committal; though the shine of the fall still lingers.

They said, the pack of them, I will not serve. The angel of suicide is one of those: a rebellious waitress. Rebellion, that's what she has to offer, to you, when you see her beckoning to you from outside the window, fifty storeys up, or the edge of the bridge, or holding something out to you, some emblem of release, soft chemical, quick metal.

Wings, of course. You wouldn't believe a thing she said if it weren't for the wings.

Poppies: Three Variations

In Flanders fields the poppies blow
Between the crosses, row on row.
That mark our place; and in the sky
The larks, still bravely singing, fly
Scarce heard amid the guns below.

— *John McCrae*

1

I had an uncle once who served *in Flanders*. Flanders, or was it France? I'm old enough to have had the uncle but not old enough to remember. Wherever, those *fields* are green again, and ploughed and harvested, though they keep throwing up rusty shells, broken skulls. *The* uncle wore a beret and marched in parades, though slowly. We always bought those felt *poppies*, which aren't even felt any more, but plastic: small red explosions pinned to your chest, like a *blow* to the heart. *Between the* other thoughts, that one *crosses* my mind. And the tiny lead soldiers in the shop windows, *row on row* of them, not lead any more, too poisonous, but every detail perfect, and from every part of the world: India, Africa, China, America. *That* goes to show, about war – in retrospect it becomes glamour, or else a game we think we could have played better. From time to time the stores *mark* them down, you can get bargains. There are some for us, too, with *our* new leafy flag, not the red rusted-blood one the men fought under. That uncle had *place*-mats with the old flag, and cups *and* saucers. The planes *in the sky* were tiny then, almost comical, like kites with wind-up motors; I've seen them in movies. The uncle said he never saw *the larks*. Too much smoke, or fog. Too much roaring, though on some mornings it was very *still*. Those were the most dangerous. You hoped you would act *bravely* when the moment came, you kept up your courage by *singing*. There was a kind of *fly* that bred in the corpses, there were thousands of them he said; and during the bombardments you could *scarce* hear yourself think. Though sometimes you *heard* things anyway: the man beside him whispered, 'Look,' and when he looked there was no more torso: just a red hole, *a* wet splotch in *mid*-air. That uncle's gone now too, the number of vets in the parade is smaller each year, they limp more. But in the windows *the* soldiers multiply, so clean and colourfully painted, with their little intricate *guns*, their shining boots, their faces, brown or pink or yellow, neither smiling nor frowning. It's strange to think how many soldiers like that have been owned over the years, loved over the years, lost over the years, in backyards or through gaps in porch floors. They're lying down there, under our feet in the garden and *below* the floorboards, armless or legless, faces worn half away, listening to everything we say, waiting to be dug up.

2

Cup of coffee, the usual morning drug. He's off jogging, told her she shouldn't be so sluggish, but she can't get organized, it involves too many things: the right shoes, the right outfit, and then worrying about how your bum looks, wobbling along the street. She couldn't do it alone anyway, she might get mugged. So instead she's sitting remembering how much she can no longer remember, of who she used to be, who she thought she would turn into when she grew up. We are the dead: that's about the only line left from *In Flanders Fields*, which she had to write out twenty times on *the* blackboard, for talking. When she was ten and thin, and now see. He says she should go vegetarian, like him, healthy as lettuce. She'd rather eat *poppies*, get the opiates straight from the source. Eat daffodils, the poisonous bulb like an onion. Or better, slice it into his soup. He'll *blow* his nose on her once too often, and then. *Between the* rock and the hard cheese, that's where she sits, inert as a prisoner, making little *crosses* on the wall, like knitting, counting the stitches *row on row, that* old trick to *mark* off the days. *Our place*, he calls this dump. He should speak for himself, she's just the mattress around here, she's just the cleaning lady, *and* when he ever lifts a finger there'll be sweet pie *in the sky*. She should burn *the* whole thing down, just for *larks; still*, however *bravely* she may talk, to herself, where would she go after that, what would she do? She thinks of the bunch of young men they saw, downtown at night, where they'd gone to dinner, his birthday. High on something, *singing* out of tune, one guy's *fly* half-open. Freedom. Catch a woman doing that, panty alert, she'd be jumped by every creep within a mile. Too late to make yourself *scarce*, once they get the skirt up. She's *heard* of a case like that, in a poolhall or somewhere. That's what keeps her in here, in this house, that's what keeps her tethered. It's not *a mid*-life crisis, which is what he says. It's fear, pure and simple. Hard to rise above it. Rise above, like a balloon or *the* cream on milk, as if all it takes is hot air or fat. Or will-power. But the reason for that fear exists, it can't be wished away. What she'd need in real life is a few *guns*. That and the technique, how to use them. And the guts, of course. She pours herself another cup of coffee. That's her big fault: she might have the gun but she wouldn't pull the trigger. She'd never be able to hit a man *below* the belt.

3

In school, when I first heard the word *Flanders* I thought it was what nightgowns were made of. And pyjamas. But then I found it was a war, more important to us than others perhaps because our grandfathers were in it, maybe, or at least some sort of ancestor. The trenches, the *fields* of mud, the barbed wire, became our memories as well. But only for a time. Photographs fade, the rain eats away at statues, *the* neurons in our brains blink out one by one, and goodbye to vocabulary. We have other things to think about, we have lives to get on with. Today I planted five *poppies* in the front yard, orangey-pink, a new hybrid. They'll go well with the marguerites. Terrorists *blow* up airports, lovers slide blindly in *between the* sheets, in the soft green drizzle my cat *crosses* the street; in the spring regatta the young men *row on, row* on, as if nothing has happened since 1913, and the crowds wave and enjoy their tall drinks with cucumber and gin. What's wrong with *that*? We can scrape by, more or less, getting from year to year with hardly a *mark* on us, as long as we know *our place*, don't mouth off too much or cause uproars. A little sex, a little gardening, flush toilets and similar discreet pleasures; *and in the sky* the satellites go over, keeping a bright eye on us. The ospreys, *the* horned *larks*, the shrikes and the woodland warblers are having a thinner time of it, though *still bravely* trying to nest in the lacunae left by pesticides, the sharp blades of the reapers. If it's *singing* you want, there's lots of that, you can tune in any time; coming out of your airplane seat-mate's earphones it sounds like a *fly* buzzing, it can drive you crazy. So can the news. Disaster sells beer, and this month hurricanes are the fashion, and famines: *scarce* this, scarce that, too little water, too much sun. With every meal you take huge bites of guilt. The excitement in the disembodied voices says: you *heard* it here first. Such *a* commotion in the *mid*-brain! Try meditation instead, be thankful for the annuals, for the smaller mercies. You listen, you listen to the moonlight, to the earthworms revelling in the lawn, you celebrate your own quick heartbeat. But below all that there's another sound, a ground swell, a drone, you can't get rid of it. It's the guns, which have never stopped, just moved around. It's the guns, still firing monotonously, bored with themselves but deadly, deadlier, deadliest, it's *the guns*, an undertone beneath each ordinary tender conversation. Say pass the sugar and you hear the guns. Say I love you. Put your ear against skin: below thought, below memory, *below* everything, the guns.

Homelanding

Where should I begin? After all, you have never been there; or if you have, you may not have understood the significance of what you saw, or thought you saw. A window is a window, but there is looking out and looking in. The native you glimpsed, disappearing behind the curtain, or into the bushes, or down the manhole in the main street – my people are shy – may have been only your reflection in the glass. My country specializes in such illusions.

115

2

Let me propose myself as typical. I walk upright on two legs, and have in addition two arms, with ten appendages, that is to say, five at the end of each. On the top of my head, but not on the front, there is an odd growth, like a species of seaweed. Some think this is a kind of fur, others consider it modified feathers, evolved perhaps from scales like those of lizards. It serves no functional purpose and is probably decorative.

My eyes are situated in my head, which also possesses two small holes for the entrance and exit of air, the invisible fluid we swim in, and one larger hole, equipped with bony protuberances called teeth, by means of which I destroy and assimilate certain parts of my surroundings and change them into my self. This is called eating. The things I eat include roots, berries, nuts, fruits, leaves, and the muscle tissues of various animals and fish. Sometimes I eat their brains and glands as well. I do not as a rule eat insects, grubs, eyeballs or the snouts of pigs, though these are eaten with relish in other countries.

3

Some of my people have a pointed but boneless external appendage, in the front, below the navel or mid-point. Others do not. Debate about whether the possession of such a thing is an advantage or disadvantage is still going on. If this item is lacking, and in its place there is a pocket or inner cavern in which fresh members of our community are grown, it is considered impolite to mention it openly to strangers. I tell you this because it is the breach of etiquette most commonly made by tourists.

In some of our more private gatherings, the absence of cavern or prong is politely overlooked, like club feet or blindness. But sometimes a prong and a cavern will collaborate in a dance, or illusion, using mirrors and water, which is always absorbing for the performers but frequently grotesque for the observers. I notice that you have similar customs.

Whole conventions and a great deal of time have recently been devoted to discussions of this state of affairs. The prong people tell the cavern people that the latter are not people at all and are in reality more akin to dogs or potatoes, and the cavern people abuse the prong people for their obsession with images of poking, thrusting, probing and stabbing. Any long object with a hole at the end, out of which various projectiles can be shot, delights them.

I myself – I am a cavern person – find it a relief not to have to worry about climbing over barbed wire fences or getting caught in zippers.

But that is enough about our bodily form.

4

As for the country itself, let me begin with the sunsets, which are long and red, resonant, splendid and melancholy, symphonic you might almost say; as opposed to the short boring sunsets of other countries, no more interesting than a light-switch. We pride ourselves on our sunsets. 'Come and see the sunset,' we say to one

118

another. This causes everyone to rush outdoors or over to the window.

Our country is large in extent, small in population, which accounts for our fear of empty spaces, and also our need for them. Much of it is covered in water, which accounts for our interest in reflections, sudden vanishings, the dissolution of one thing into another. Much of it however is rock, which accounts for our belief in Fate.

In summer we lie about in the blazing sun, almost naked, covering our skins with fat and attempting to turn red. But when the sun is low in the sky and faint, even at noon, the water we are so fond of changes to something hard and white and cold and covers up the ground. Then we cocoon ourselves, become lethargic, and spend much of our time hiding in crevices. Our mouths shrink and we say little.

Before this happens, the leaves on many of our trees turn blood-red or lurid yellow, much brighter and more exotic than the interminable green of jungles. We find this change beautiful. 'Come and see the leaves,' we say, and jump into our moving vehicles and drive up and down past the forests of sanguinary trees, pressing our eyes to the glass.

We are a nation of metamorphs.

Anything red compels us.

5

Sometimes we lie still and do not move. If air is still going in and out of our breathing holes, this is called sleep. If not, it is called death. When a person has achieved death, a kind of picnic is held, with music, flowers and food. The person so honoured, if in one piece, and not, for instance, in shreds or falling apart, as they do if exploded or a long time drowned, is dressed in becoming clothes and lowered into a hole in the ground, or else burnt up.

These customs are among the most difficult to explain to strangers. Some of our visitors, especially the young ones, have never heard of death and are bewildered. They think that death is simply one more of our illusions, our mirror tricks; they cannot understand why, with so much food and music, the people are sad.

But you will understand. You too must have death among you. I can see it in your eyes.

6

I can see it in your eyes. If it weren't for this I would have stopped trying long ago, to communicate with you in this halfway language which is so difficult for both of us, which exhausts the throat and fills the mouth with sand; if it weren't for this I would have gone away, gone back. It's this knowledge of death, which we share, where we overlap. Death is our common ground. Together, on it, we can walk forward.

By now you must have guessed: I come from another planet. But I will never say to you, take me to your leaders. Even I – unused to your ways though I am –

would never make that mistake. We ourselves have such beings among us, made of cogs, pieces of paper, small disks of shiny metal, scraps of coloured cloth. I do not need to encounter more of them.

Instead I will say, take me to your trees. Take me to your breakfasts, your sunsets, your bad dreams, your shoes, your nouns. Take me to your fingers; take me to your deaths.

These are worth it. These are what I have come for.

Third Handed

The third hand is the one stamped in bear's grease and ochre, in charcoal and blood, on the walls of five-thousand-year-old caves; and in blue, on the doorposts, to ward off evil. It hangs in silver on a chain around the neck, signalling with its thumb; or index finger extended, and with its golden wrist attached to an ebony stick, it strokes its way along the textural footpath, from Aleph to Omega. In churches it lurks in reliquaries, bony and bejewelled, or appears abruptly from fresco clouds, enormous and stern and significant, loud as a shout: Sin! Less elegant, banal even, and stencilled on a metal plate, it bosses us around: *Way Out*, it orders. *Up Here. Way Down.*

But these are merely pictures of it: roles, disguises,

captured images, that in no way confine it. Do pictures of love confine love?

(The man and the woman walk down the street, hand in passionate hand; but whose hand is it really? It's the third hand each one holds, not the beloved's. It's the third hand that joins them together, the third hand that keeps them apart.)

The third hand is neither left nor right, dexter nor sinister. Consider the man who is caught in the act, red-handed as they say. He proclaims his innocence, and why not believe him? *What axe?* he says. *I didn't know what I was doing, it wasn't me, and look, my hands are clean!* No one notices the third hand creeping away painfully on its fingers, like a stepped-on crab, trailing raw blood from its severed wrist.

But that happens only to those who have disowned it, who have cut it off and nailed it to a board and shut it up in a wall-safe or a strongbox. It's light-fingered, the hand of a thief in the night; it will always get out, it will never hold still. It writes, and having written, moves. Moves on, dissolving, dissolving boundaries.

Vacant spaces belong to it, the vowel O, all blank pages, the number zero, the animals wolf and mole, the hour before birth and the minute after death, the loon, the owl, and all white flowers. The third hand opens doors, and closes them thoughtfully behind you. It is the other two that busy themselves with what goes on in the room.

The third hand is the hand the magician holds behind his back, while showing you the other two, candid and empty. *The hand is quicker than the eye*, he says. Notice that it's *hand*, singular. Only one. The third.

And when you walk through the snow, in the blizzard, growing cold and then unaccountably warmer, as night descends and sleep numbs you and you know you are lost, it's the third hand that slips confidingly into your own, a small hand, the hand of a child, leading you onward.

Death Scenes

I want to get the rose-bushes in first. I like just sitting there. Last night there was a firefly. Can you imagine?

He said I could heal myself. He told me over the phone. He said, I can hear it in your voice. You should meditate on light for three minutes every day, and drink the leaves of cabbages, the leaves right next to the outer ones. Put them in a blender. Some garlic, too. You'll pee green, but you'll heal. You know, it actually worked, for a while.

This is not attractive. I know it isn't, especially the hair. What do I want? I want you to talk about normal things.

I know I look like hell. But it's still me in here. What do I want? I want you to talk about normal things. No I

127

don't. I want you to look me in the eye and say, *I know you're dying*. But for Christ's sake don't make me console you.

I said, get the *fuck* out. This has nothing to do with my *fucking* attitude. Of course I'm bitter! Get out or I'll throw something at you. Where's the bedpan? You know I don't mean it. Christ I'd like a drink. Well, why not, eh?

No, don't. Don't hug me. It hurts.

I want to see what comes up, in the spring. Damn squirrels, they eat the bulbs. Mothballs are supposed to work.

If you want to cry, do it around the corner where she can't see you.

It's time for you to go home.

Something went wrong, we don't know what. We think you should come down at once.

— Can't you do something? It isn't her, it isn't her! She looks like the Pillsbury Doughboy, she's all swollen up, I can't stand it!

— It's not bothering her, she's in a coma.

— I don't believe in comas! She can hear, she can see everything! If you're going to talk about *death*, let's go down to the coffee-shop.

It's cruel, it's cruel, she's never going to wake up! She can't get back into her body, and if she did she'd hate it! Can't somebody pull the plug?

I knew she'd died when the ashtray broke. It cracked right across. It was the one she gave me. I knew she was right there! It was her way of letting me know.

Glorious scenes. *Glorious* scenes! Nobody made scenes like hers. Vulgar as all-get-out. Of course, she would always apologize afterwards. She needn't have done. Not to me.

What I miss is what she'd say. What she would have said. That's the difference: you have to put everything into the past conditional. *Bereft*, you might call it. Not her word, though – too po-faced. *That* was her word.

I went over there, did a little weeding. It's fading though, what she looked like exactly. I can remember her tone of voice, but not her voice. It's funny the way you keep on talking to people. It's as if they could hear.

Four Small Paragraphs

For Mr. Flat

This is the landscape where he came to rest: the earth, ochre and rust, that has been used and reused, passed through mouth and stomach and gut and bone, and out again into earth and then into stem and bud and ripe fruit, then harvested and bruised and fermented for a moment of warmth; the pruned vines like twisted fists, the unclipped ones with their long yellowish intertwined fingernails, like those of potatoes in the dark; and the light inside everything, oozing up from the furrows like juice from a cut peach, glistening along the leaves like the slippery backs of snails, like licked lips. When it rains, the dust of the Sahara 611s from the south wind, spotting the white plastic patio chairs at the *tabac* with dried blood. Higher up are the limestone mountains, dry and covered with tough and pungent shrubs, the *maquis* they're called, and gullied by time and sparse as aphorism. He liked the harshness of the sun here, or so he said.

In the restaurant he was known as Monsieur Terrasse, an alias to deceive the tourists while he ate his dinner. I almost said *terrorists*. Famous people don't wish to be interrupted while chewing, or watched closely while they do it. Neither does anyone else, but there's less likelihood. In English he was *Mr. Patio*. Many things are more romantic in French, the word *odour* for instance. *Camus* translates as plain *flat*, but he wouldn't have minded.

The books in the brick-and-board bookshelves, dismantled, reconstructed, dispersed, it must be thirty years ago, are turning yellow and then brown, crumbling at the edges like fallen leaves, consuming themselves from within. There's the same odour, a slow acrid burning. Uncompromising, he wished to be; and clear, like the desert light.

On All Souls' Day the dead are tended. Here it's a duty. The graves are weeded, and huge bubbles of bright paint bloom beside them: chrysanthemums, purple and orange, yellow and red; and china dahlias too, the colour of last year's lipstick, and brittle pansies chipped by hail. What he himself has been given is not ornate. Squareness and greyness, the elegance of plainsong, no mottoes. No gilded mementoes, no picture of him in a glassy oval, that quizzical face with its simian postwar brush-cut. What do I remember most clearly, from all those acrid pages? The scene in which a man spits on a woman's naked body, because she has been unfaithful. What did he mean to convey, to me? Something about betrayal, or else about women's bodies? He isn't telling. An abrupt bush is what he has, with dark cryptic foliage, one of the mountain shrubs. No hope, no armfuls of petals. *This is what there is*, he says, or fails to say. *You are what you do. Don't expect mercy*. Later, when I went back, someone had left six withering real roses in a kitchen jar.

We Want It All

What we want of course is the same old story. The trees pushing out their leaves, fluttering them, shucking them off, the water thrashing around in the oceans, the tweedling of the birds, the unfurling of the slugs, the worms vacuuming dirt. The zinnias and their pungent slow explosions. We want it all to go on and go on again, the same thing each year, monotonous and amazing, just as if we were still behaving ourselves, living in tents, raising sheep, slitting their throats for God's benefit, refusing to invent plastics. For unbelief and bathrooms you pay a price. If apples were the Devil's only bait we'd still be able to call our souls our own, but then the prick threw indoor plumbing into the bargain and we were doomed. Now

135

we use up a lot of paper telling one another how to conserve paper, and the sea fills up with killer coffee cups, and we worry about the sun and its ambivalent rays.

When will it all cave in? The sky, I mean; our networks; our intricate pretensions. We were too good at what we did, at being fruitful, at multiplying, and now there's too much breathing. We eat dangerous foods, our shit glows in the dark, the cells of our bodies turn on us like sharks. Every system is self-limiting. Will we solve ourselves as the rats do? With war, with plagues, with mass starvation? These thoughts come with breakfast, like the juice from murdered fruits. Your depression, my friend, is the revenge of the oranges.

But we still find the world astounding, we can't get enough of it; even as it shrivels, even as its many lights flicker and are extinguished (the tigers, the leopard frogs, the plunging dolphin flukes), flicker and are extinguished, by us, by us, we gaze and gaze. Where do you draw the line, between love and greed? We never did know, we always wanted more. We want to take it all in, for one last time, we want to eat the world with our eyes.

Better than the mouth, my darling. Better than the mouth.

Dance of the Lepers

Who knows whether there could be such a thing? Possibly lepers do not dance, or are unable to. On the other hand, possibly they do. Somebody must know.

In the Dance of the Lepers, the lepers were not real. That is, they did not have leprosy. On the contrary. These lepers were healthy, able-bodied and young. They were dancers. But they were pretending to be lepers, and since I always believe in surfaces, I believed that they were real.

The pretended, real dance of the lepers took place on a stage. It was Christmas up there. The music was quick, with nasal horns and light-fingered drums. People in medieval costumes whirled about. Muscular beggars were there, slender maidens in pointed caps with trailing veils, a stately prince, a voluptuous Gypsy, a witty fool.

Everything you might require. Daydream ingredients. Take-out romance.

Then the lights dimmed and the music slowed, and the lepers entered. There were five of them; they held onto one another, to various parts of their various bodies, because they could not see. They were dressed in white strips of cloth wound round and around them, around their bodies and also around their hands and heads. They had no faces, only this blunt cloth.

They looked like animated mummies from an old horror film. They looked like living bed-sheets. They looked like war casualties. They looked like cocoons. They looked like people you once knew very well, whose names you've forgotten. They looked like your own face in the steam-covered mirror after a bath, your own face temporarily nameless. They looked like aphasia. They looked like an ad for bandages. They looked like a bondage photo. They looked erotic. They looked obliterated. They looked like a sad early death.

The music they danced to was filled with the ringing of bells. In fact they carried little bells, little iron bells, or so I seem to remember. That was to warn people: stay away from the lepers. Or: stay away from the dance. Dancing can be dangerous.

What about their dance? There is very little I can tell you about that. One thing is certain: it was not a tap-dance. Also: no pirouettes.

It was a dance of supplication, a numb dance, a dance of hopelessness and resignation. Also: a dance of continuation, a dance of going on despite everything, a stubborn dance. An awkward, hampered dance. A fluid, graceful dance. A clumsy, left-footed, infinitely skilful dance. A cynical and disgusted dance, a dance of worship, naive and joyful. A dance.

Ah lepers. If you can dance, even you, why not the rest of us?

Good Bones

1

You have good bones, they used to say, and I paid no attention. What did I care about good bones, then? I was more concerned with what was covering them. I was more concerned with lust, and pimples. The bones were backdrop.

Now they are growing into their own, those bones. Flesh diminishes, giving way to bedrock. Structural principles. What you need is the right light, to blot out the wrinkles, the incidentals. The right shade, the right amount of sun, and see, out come the bones, the good bones, the bones come out like flowers.

2

Them bones, them bones, them dry bones, them and their good connections; we sang them over once around the campfire, those gleeful strutters to the Word of the Lord, or to our own hands clapping. Behind each face, each lovely body in its plaid shirt, soft bum on hard granite, I could guess the Hallowe'en skeleton, white and one-dimensional, a chalk bonehead drawn on a blackboard; a zombie, a brief *memento mori*, dragged out for burning, like a heretic, flanked by the torches of the incandescent marshmallows.

Our voices made short work of them, them bones. Tossed on the bonfire they flared up like butter, and went out and were dismissed. *You are my sunshine*, we sang, though not to them. We nestled closer, jellifying each other, some of us boneless.

So much for death. So much for death, at that time, there.

3

This is the cemetery. The good bones are in here, the bad bones are out there, beyond the church wall, beyond the pale, unsanctified.

The bad bones behaved badly, perhaps because of bad blood, bad luck, bad childhoods. Anyway, they did not treat their bodies well. Walked them over cliff edges, jumped them off bell-towers. Tried to fly. Broke things.

The good bones lie snug under their tidy monuments. They have been given brooches to wear, signet rings, poems carved on stone, marble urns, citations. Circlets of bright hair. They have been worthy and dutiful, they deserve it. That's what it says here: the last word.

The bad bones have been bad, so they are better left unsaid. They are better left unsaying. But they were never happy, they always wanted more, they were always hungry. They can smell the words, the words coming out of your mouth all warm and yeasty.

They want some words of their own. They'll be back.

4

This is my friend, these are her bones, these ashes we pour out under the tulips. When she fell down on the sidewalk her hip-bone shattered. It was hollow in there, eaten away, like a tree with ants. Bone meal.

They put her in the hospital and I went to see her. I'm terrified, she said, but it's sort of interesting. My turds are white, like bird turds. It's calcium. I'm dissolving myself, I'm shitting bones. I guess you can do worse than be fertilizer. Other things can grow.

We are both fond of gardens.

5

Today I speak to my bones as I would speak to a dog. I want to go up the stairs, I tell them. Up, up, up, with one leg dragging. Is the ache deep in the bones, this elusive pain? Does that mean it will rain? Good bones, *good* bones, I coax, wondering how to reward them; if they will sit up for me, beg, roll over, do one more trick, once more.

There. We're at the top. *Good* bones! Good *bones*! Keep on going.

Wilderness Tips

Margaret Atwood

A leathery bog-man transforms an old love affair; a
sweet, gruesome gift is sent to the wife of an ex-lover;
landscape paintings are haunted by the ghost of a
young girl. This dazzling collection of ten short stories
takes us into familiar Atwood territory to reveal the
logic of irrational behaviour and the many textures
lying beneath ordinary life.

'Atwood is a writer of importance, with a deep
understanding of human behaviour, a beautiful
understated style, and rarest of all, a broad scope'
Marilyn French

Murder in the Dark

Margaret Atwood

These short fictions and prose poems are beautifully bizarre: bread can no longer be thought of as wholesome comforting loaves; the pretensions of the male chef are subjected to a light roasting; a poisonous brew is concocted by cynical five year olds; and knowing when to stop is of deadly importance in a game of Murder in the Dark.

'Direct, unpretentious, humorous' *Sunday Times*

Moral Disorder

Margaret Atwood

'Atwood entices us to flip through the photo album of a Canadian woman who closely resembles herself. Come here, sit beside me, she seems to say. Then she takes us on an emotional journey through loneliness, love, loss and old age'
Sarah Emily Miano, *The Times*

This is Margaret Atwood at her very finest.

'Funny, touching, beady-eyed, slouchily elegant, giving us family life in all its horrors. The secret resentments and alignments – difficult siblings, unfair parents, hopeless yearnings and rage – are funny to read about, hellish to experience. Atwood makes it look so easy, doing what she does best: tenderly dissecting the human heart . . . She is a marvellous writer' Lee Langley, *Daily Mail*

virago

To buy any of our books and to find out more
about Virago Press and Virago Modern Classics,
our authors and titles, as well as events and
book club forum, visit our websites

www.virago.co.uk
www.littlebrown.co.uk

and follow us on Twitter

@ViragoBooks

To order any Virago titles p & p free in the UK,
please contact our mail order supplier on:

+ 44 (0)1832 737525

Customers not based in the UK should contact
the same number for appropriate postage
and packing costs.